# LICK OF SENSE

*Winner of the 2000 Marianne Moore Poetry Prize*

*The Marianne Moore Poetry Prize*
*was established in 1991 by Helicon Nine Editions,*
*and is awarded annually to a previously unpublished*
*manuscript chosen by a distinguished writer*
*through an open nationwide competition.*

*The judge for 2000 was Alicia Ostriker.*

# LICK OF SENSE

## POEMS

Suzanne Rhodenbaugh

*Suzanne Rhodenbaugh*

Winner of the 2000 Marianne Moore Poetry Prize
Selected by Alicia Ostriker

*St. Louis, Missouri*
*May, 2005*

HELICON NINE EDITIONS
KANSAS CITY & LOS ANGELES

*Acknowledgments appear on page 84.*

Cover illustration: Woodcut by Sigue E. Garson, 1930.
Cover and book design: Tim Barnhart

Helicon Nine Editions, a non-profit small press, is funded in part by
the National Endowment for the Arts, a federal agency,
the Kansas Arts Commission and the Missouri Arts Council, state agencies.

MAC     Kansas Arts Commission
MISSOURI ARTS COUNCIL

Library of Congress Cataloging -in-Publication Data

Rhodenbaugh, Suzanne.
    Lick of sense : poems / Suzanne Rhodenbaugh.-- 1st ed.
        p. cm.
    "Winner of the 2000 Marianne Moore Poetry Prize selected by Alicia Ostriker."
    ISBN 1-884235-33-6 (pbk. : alk. paper)
    I. Title.

PS3568.H542 L54 2001
811'.54--dc21

Manufactured in the United States of America
FIRST EDITION

HELICON NINE EDITIONS
KANSAS CITY AND LOS ANGELES

*To Tom Rhodenbaugh,*
*my love for twenty-five years*

and in memory of these friends:

Avedis Donabedian
Aimee Gibson
George Goldstein
Julia Singer

and granddaddy Papa: Elisha Dillard Douglas
of Georgia and Florida, 1880-1964

# Table of Contents

# I

"All my children are smart,
and not a one's got a lick of sense."

—Mamma

# The Acolyte of Grooming

The monkey in me grasped mutual grooming
signifies love, and has a calming effect.
Plus comes in handy for prickly problems
not resolvable by sole salvation:
big lobs of thin dead skin on the back, say,
after a bad sunburn. Like a kid
in a Shake 'n Bake ad, I helped:
plucked eyebrows and tweezed out splinters,
squeezed blackheads, brushed thick dark coarse-

crowned heads. The youngest and lowest ranking,
I didn't receive the devotion
but made suntanned brunette elder sisters
more beautiful than they already were.
And then I'd get to watch the getting-ready
beyond the basic grooming: toenail painting,
for one thing, the color called tomato red.
The shaving of legs and armpits. The washing
of hair in milk or beer. The pancake make-up,
the cherry rouge, the big dark Maybelline lips—

the whole ceremony of getting
a man—going out with him in a car at night
and smooching, the quick jump then
to a wedding: the mystery's exact trajectory
I didn't quite get,
but I knew it all began with grooming
head to toe, and topping off with Evening in Paris
from a dark blue bottle—the odor,
as Mamma called it, could throttle a bull.

# Jitterbugging the Bottom

We pulled back the big claw-footed round oak table,
the one years later Peggy and Katherine
fought over, ruining one complete Christmas,
only to mean Katherine took that thing
and put it in her basement in Atlanta, let it get
stained and warped, then sold it out of the family.

But that night we still had it and we moved it.
The chairs pushed back, we were ready.
Fats, Chuck Berry, Jerry Lee Lewis, Bo Diddley,
Elvis Presley: all the absolute best

we had on 45's, in a pink and black carrying case
made expressly for taking your music
to parties. We could dance. I mean we could
dance, and the house was just full of Bill's buddies,
big sexy young guys crazy to boogie and Lord we did,
so hard we shook the plumbing pipes loose from the house.

Our house was built on short stilts, on a bedrock
of sand, with a network of springs under that.
If you'd gone down under it far enough
you could've swum from Tampa clear to Crystal River.

(And come up and found yourself looking
smack-dab in the faces of manatees
which—Friends of the Earth, excuse me—don't in any way
look like mermaids, or mysterious sirens of the sea.
In fact up close they look like blobs:
you can't tell their ends from their beginnings.)

So in a house where anger got mopped up with mad,
one June night in '55 we shook the pipes loose.
And this is how stories get started: we fill up
with magic and beauty what we won't otherwise preserve.

# The Causeway

The Skyliners played that Saturday night
we pulled up close to the old beach hall
where Tampa, the earth as we knew it,
ends, and the causeway starts.

*Lavender blue, dilly dilly*:
the last slow dance.
We were near to fainting
with the heat and the fuchsia
oleander and the rank, raw
smell of the beach, you
wiry and rangy in a tailfinned coupe
with me, my dark hair swept back
in a ponytail, blonde streaks
at both my temples, my blue
polished cotton halter-neck dress,
my toenails painted sugarpink.

The moon over Tampa Bay,
and the silver line of the causeway
joining one slim beach to another miles away
I lay with later at home.

I spread out on a beach bag
dried opalescent
coquina shells, and put them in
designs: coquina rings
quiescent as seed pearls,
too tiny for hearing the tide
of pain, blood, babies,
a world all over me,
I'd heard in the car
and halted. I took so much
in my hands then, and made
whatever dream comes true.

Not a bar of "Lavender Blue,"
not a glimpse of the blossom
of the sweet oleander doesn't
bring it on home to me.

# Early Red Bride

I was born baldly red, fed maraschino cherries
and strawberries—real Florida strawberries
red to the tip and half a hand big—I got
Red Eye swimming at the lake, ate Red Hots
at the movies Saturday afternoons oh I wore
a red hibiscus in my hair and in a halter dress
did jitterbug under strung lanterns

of the schoolyard. Under the turning mirrored
globe of the ballroom, in my red
velvet sheath dress I slow-danced,
and so married, still in my teens, and rubies
hung in my long-pierced ears.

# Our Songs
# Beginning with If

*If you've got the money, honey,*
*I've got the time...*

*If this train's*
*runnin' right, I'll be home*
*tomorrow night...*

Remember how we changed
*right* to *wild*? How we made a sweet
double dollop by changing
*money* to *honey*? We sang
blues and hillbilly music so often

conditional. Funny, isn't it, how *if* qualifies
what could be true, and makes things so hard
and complex, yet rises again
and again, from what some folks consider
low music? It's true, like Willie said,

*You were always on my mind.* And it's true,
my thoughts were lusty and lowdown,
like Tina Turner singing *What's love*
*got to do with it?*—That song got all mixed up
with a little longing for the night
we sang along with *Someday soon,*
*goin' with you, someday soon...*

Which the odds are, I will never do.
Because we're settled, older, married
to others, we've got to content ourselves
with that old-time croony placid ballad

*If I loved you, words wouldn't come*
*in an easy way...* That song tells it
right. It never admits, not fully,

the love, the love that stays
conditional to the very end, and yet,

I can remember the whole thing, can't you?

II

# Having Given Up My Baby for Adoption

From the window of a slow-moving train
I saw a dog on top of a building
many stories high. I could see its sound—
its frantic bark—as it ran from one
edge to another and looked down. Unable to provide
on top of all that steel and stone,
unable even to make itself heard,
it was alone and thoroughly terrified.

It was not a complicated dog
in love with the transcendent
who'd made its own way near to God.
An ironic God wasn't present.

Cruelty or willful neglect,
this was something human someone meant.

# The Shed

There's a low windowless shed
in the bottomland of Dwale, Kentucky,
flatcamp on the muddy creek they call Big Sandy River.

Pawpaw trees are bearing heavily this year,
daylilies grow up wild everywhere in patches
and the kudzu spirals up the pines.

But the shed sits in the heat,
the scramble-boarded,
padlocked shed.

A creature's stored alone in that shed,
a beagle hound for stud
living out a lifetime there.

In winter, the wind comes down through the hollows
and blows across the bottomland. First frost,
the shit-covered ground grows hard,
and the hound lives on, a kind of life,
and spring sometimes creek and mountain run-off
move over the bottomland.

The hound lives on, how many years.

They say the man who owns that hound has forgotten
hunts, the proving ground for hounds,
and now the fee for stud goes unpaid too—
he's forgotten why he keeps that hound,
what the profit is in it. Still,

the dog stays, it's that man's way
to pen the seed that will make other hounds for hunt
in a windowless, padlocked shed.
He bakes his dog. He makes him ripe.

And if a bitch in heat were brought,
would the stored seed fester?
Has the hound died down into a version of himself,
so much he fears daylight?
Is he crippled, is he mean, is he
whimpering for kindness so softly the sound
comes like a slight breeze in the pawpaw trees?
And who will hear, or care?

The man may be the limping version of a man
across the road, the one with a meat-red cluster
of scar tissue stump where a hand had been.
Maybe the hound
took the hand, and ravaged the leg on that side.

Or maybe it was the old story:
the price the mountains take
to take the coal.

And maybe after years at low coal and hard times
the man wanted not even the hunt,
the tear in the white-tailed deer
for his pick-up hood—not even that,
but a price for stud.

And then that price forgotten,
and only the man's way going on.

I know we all lock something up,
a kind of life,
in heat and dirt and dark.

The price we've already paid is reason
something's going on, for years.

Each dog in us is
someway twisted,
not let to run
and held close by
in the sickest version of ourselves.

But I'm talking here about a living dog,
a beagle pup,
and not some got-up metaphor.

I'm talking here about a living dog.

# November Had Been in the Shenandoah

Mounds of rusted crownvetch had fallen
to a sallow field.

Ringed by a fretwork of briartrees,
a mare had stood attuned, and still.

Tan, some grey in her muzzle.
Blonde had been in her mane.

Her back had dipped in the sway,
from years, of a rider.

She had stayed in the blanched
stubble of the field. Had listened.

# Nathan

I lay on the narrow bed in the cool dark house on the hill
high above the Ohio,
listening to the barges on the river and the coal trucks
coming and going along the river in West Virginia,
and ached for an old man in a dark hospital
on a cliff above
a dirty little coal mining town on the Ohio River.

What could he think if he woke,
alone, in the dark?

What if I left my bed
and slipped barefooted
through the tall narrow houses
hunching on the valley floor,
and climbed ravines
up behind the hospital,
and slipped past the horse-faced nurses
and came to his side
and took his hand
and held it
and offered to take it—
the tremor, the being a burden,
the knowing in the dark
you've become something to be hefted—

would he shift his ragged eyes
and turn his head
and tell me to go back to the river,
to the woods,
to my cool dark cage
and leave him with his,
which isn't mine     which isn't my dying?

# Hazel Agrees to Talk

You know it's a rainy night, the hoot owl shift,
and my man's three miles under
but I'll talk to you—yeah, I'll tell you.

Hear that rumble? That's the coal trucks.
See those barges on the river? They go by
black houses, hospitals, old black banks.

This coal dust settles, hauling coal,
and everybody mines,
might say the doctors and the lawyers

mine the pain—outsiders too,
I'll tell you. You take my house—
wedged in the Valley

with the others—still owned
by the company in Wheeling—yeah,
the coal camps. Now our women are large

but our men are some bones and black spit—
fingers gone in every union hall.
And the crows' feet of some men

are always black—comes of working
seam in low roof. Talk about your broken men.
How bout thirty years of daylight, gone?

Yeah we call rats bless-ed—that means there's air,
and yeah, the mules used to go blind down there, yeah,
I'll talk to you.

# Winnie Cotton's Husband

Asked to speak for a job for me
back then, when I needed one bad,
he said "I can't speak a piece.
Times are hard here like everywhere else.
Don't lay your troubles on me."

Winnie Cotton's husband closed down
to me. I guess he'd got harder as years
clutched by—daylight, midnight,
hoot owl shift—I just know he died
at the mine—Winnie Cotton's husband,

when his heart acted up, and him just fifty-nine.
He wasn't always a friend to me
but he was a friend of mine—
Winnie Cotton's husband, when his heart
acted up, and that was near all the time.

# The Carbide Lamp

He'd had to buy it with scrip.
Back then you had to get your own: real brass
he'd cleaned the coal dust from each night.

Now it centers an arrangement someone made him
when he finally got that pension. Some celebration:
the old lamp sits squarely on a board

tacked with dried fern, trumpet mushroom,
eucalyptus. He won't cry or say a word.
When his children drive out of the slag heaps

and boneypiles of Nanty Glo, he'll be alone
remembering when the heading collapsed in the Colver shaft
or the time scabs almost got past the pickets at No. 9.

Nowdays the young fellows show up drunk for shift,
and skip the meetings of the local altogether.
Hell he was there

when the thing was made—
by God the *Union*. He can touch it
with his two stubs, and his eight fingers.

# In Memory of Rudy and John

This was in our full life, with a lot to go on
and history alive—that picture on the wall,
the three of us in blackened coveralls
that day we went down in the Colver Mine.

They took me the hard way, I guess.
In water and muck and cold and dark
we crouched and crawled two miles.
"You afraid?" they'd ask. "Hell no" I'd lie.

Portal to mineface and back in low roof,
we came up filthy and haggard at dusk
on Ebensburg Road. John pointed with a stub
the mines had made

and Rudy could hardly tamp his delight:
white-tailed deer in the headlamp beams!
We watched that quick life bound and flee
like we'd come to the deepest part of the mine.

III

# Back Travel

Long ago the back was flat,
but then someone imagined
a creek bed down the middle—dry gulch,
and those who wanted to lick it called it

the body's Mississippi—
the sweat on the left rolls east,
the eastern sweat rolls west
from the two felled trunks laid side by side,

there the pipe is set
between the raised crop rows,
there the long plait of nerve moves
down the body's continent,

a design God made after thinking about a back,
a hand moving over it.
When we danced and I lay last night
my three longest fingers in that space

and lightly rested my thumb on your eastern side
and smallest finger on your west
I thought: forget history, anything
this good should have a name.

# Wahoo's Whitewater Wrafting:

the name of the enterprise
tacked on the schoolbus/office
so we said: What the hell,
let's do it. Turned out Wahoo
was the dude's name—this is how
my son would tell that adventure—
little misrepresentative,
my husband would say, not
really true my daughter
would report and I would call it
a goddamn outright lie
that creaky parents, and two kids
way underage, were prepared
for that adventure but
we put down our money—cash.
We said Wahoo, we are ready.

At the head of the Nolichucky
River Gorge, Wahoo's assistant,
a credentialed guy with life
saving skills, commenced to train us.
He said: Paddle like hell to live.
Right, we said, we gotcha.
On a raft with missionary-looking
elder folks and this tall blonde
skinny assistant, we got about
half mile down the Gorge
when our boy said That guy's
in the water. What? I said. Who?
Oh the guy who's steering this thing:
he fell out at Devil's Rapids.

Well when he got to the boulders
we were stuck between, he warned us

severely: Anyone falls out, don't
hang on—most likely that'll
hurt em more and it could
kill em—smash em on a rock
or somethin—just let em
float and catch up with the raft.
Oh God this was
way too much adventure,
this going down Class 6 rapids,
we learned later, that means:
Sucker, do it only if you're
prepared to meet your Maker
but we were hell-bent
for adventure—I was finding
reserves of skill in myself—
the speeches made a strong
impression—when our little girl
fell out and boy
hung on the precise exact
opposite to our instructions.

Long story short, we saved her:
kind of adventure
seemed exciting later
but at the time was scary
and also I forgot to mention,
in case you're not
familiar with the general
area, we were in *Deliverance* country,
in our own book/movie
with children, a certified
life saver, two preachers
and, beside us in a kayak,
going backwards down Devil's Drop
just to see if they could,
Wahoo and his girlfriend Pretty.

If they could've
taken away our parents' licenses
that would've been the day to do it
though to our credit
we were only giving an adventure
to the kids to remember and Jesus
I was paddling hard and steady,
I wasn't losing
a bit of concentration. Well,

finally it was lunch
on a rocky beachhead: white
bread and peanut butter, cherry
Koolaid I think I remember
clearly Wahoo didn't expend too much
on the "hand-packed lunches"
and the preachers, two
watersoaked increasingly
silent geezers, were looking
older and tireder and the afternoon's
mostly a blur: names
all started with Devil
is what I remember
of the rills and the rapids
and the whirlpools, and the goddamn
waterfalls: Devil's Turbulence,
Devil's-Own-Row-to-Hoe,
Devil's-Water-Getcha-If-You-
Stop Paddling and I didn't,
I was intent on this
adventure and the sun
was going down early
when we landed, at last,
in Tennessee:

quiet country town—white frame

porches, picket fences,
a regular dream of a
safe place but
at the 7-11,
stocking up on fare
for the bus ride back, Wahoo
started in on a story:

This town's where, in 1910,
they hung an elephant.
Yessir, I shit you not.
Poor thing sat on a kid—
by mistake of course but
folks in this town
are crazy. Had a trial and found him guilty.
Couldn't find a tree big enough—
brought in a crane and did it.
This town is little but it's
famous and they don't
cotton to outsiders—
best if we be gone by dark. Well,

we stopped just once
for what was left of our adventure—
another roadside entrepreneur,
this one selling
pornographic houseplants:
little men with cactus cocks.
I bought one and asked about
tax on the thing.
Fellow selling said:
I don't truck with taxes.
He wore overalls, wore a cap that said
Who Gives a Shit? which I did,
plenty, let me tell you,
that whole adventure

with my man and my kids and Pretty,
the state-licensed, trained
life saver, two preachers
and of course Wahoo,
I was paying mind to paddle.

# At Quaker Meeting, The Spirit Dog

A big black dog lay in the middle of the silent circle
of Friends, gave a few baleful thumps of his tail,
loudly sighed and settled back into a boredom

ever so profound. I loved that dog that day.
He made me want to laugh out loud that all our assemblage
of lawyers, and administrators, and other purveyors

of a world we tried to love and question both—
all goodwill, Volvos and beansprouts—were waiting,
in silence, for The Spirit. It seemed nothing like The Spirit

would move in a city living room with hayrakes on the walls
for ornament, a room just beige to its core, though we were
sincere and earnest people, repudiating

knit toilet paper holders and vinyl covers over couches
lasting a whole lifetime's marriage and beyond and our parents'
more talky religions. One woman spoke once, something about

discovering herself. It didn't seem like The Spirit.
Then a fellow not trying to make big a little thought he had said
That dog right in the middle of us here

is beautiful. I love that dog. He lit up with his saying
the shiny coat and curling tail and floppy iridescent ears
of the dog, who raised his head in that open, goony way

a dog hoping for a romp will do, and a plain awkward woman
in a business suit grabbed the platter of pastries, pale
almond crescents for the after-meeting coffee, took off

her high heels, ran with the dog out the door and, all the way
down the long driveway, for the leaping, eating, hugely
happy big black dog, hung those moons in the daylight sky.

## Suzanne's Metaphysic,
## An Explanation to George,
## With Interruptions, The Complete Text

Start with a human footprint,
just one of them—small
in a large territory, as in a modern
oblique greeting card of wit
or your own grandchild's
tiny mark at the beach.
The main thing is the small mark
and the vastness surrounding it.
The print is dark blue
on a white grounding.
                      Where's the other foot?
It is apparent
that without both feet
there will be no movement
and further a sort of implied
crippling. So let us
put both feetprint in.
Now the little stonemarks of the toes
and the twisted hourglasses
that omit the insteps
are both there. Still
the field is largely white
but the means to travel are there.
At this point: a dilemma.
Should we bring in
another pair of feet,
diminishing this human's
singular importance?
Or should we begin a trail
across the sand in lowtide?

Perhaps another species' prints
should approach or be evident—
possibly a moose's (if we want
hilarity) or a bear's
if we're deadly serious.
                Other things make their mark
                but not in prints.
                For instance, snake-squiggles.
Let us keep it human prints:
two feet, dark blue, white ground.
                What about the legless?
                This could be a veteran,
                 or a leper.
Two feet are necessary—the prints
profoundly noticeable.
The legs are marching in place,
driving the marks deeper into the ground
for—no mistaking—this
is a modern person.
                Can't the feet walk
                or fall in love or something?
I will say one tentative toe
begins to make an arc
out from the epicenter.
                What about leg irons?
                Maybe this is a prisoner or a slave
                left on shore. Irons weigh feet down
                and make even deeper footholes.
Let us remember
the toe designing
its ingenious circle.
Then the other foot begins to wobble,
leading the feet-mover to discern
movement is dangerous
and obscures the prints' clarity,
which is after all our subject.

Is it getting cold? Is it
hot? Has a typhoon
been sighted offshore?
There is some wind
blows the white grounding about,
so that the porous sand
begins to blur
those tiny
so distinct blue
human prints.

Are there any of those
blue-footed boobie birds
waddling by?

# A Bird Lives in My Grocery Store

A metallic coffee brown just made
for feathers, he balances—no problem—
on the girders over the aisles,
lower than the giant fluorescent grids
but clearly out of reach.
                         And when he flies!
What a stir in the reaches of my grocery store!
The air currents get going in the metal rafters.
Even the cabbage leaves—those New England shut-ins—
lift a little when the air struts
winnow down to the produce.

Today I took my first notice.
I walked direct to the manager—a middling
bleached blonde woman in fuchsia knit,
a sort of living pomegranate—
and said apologetically but straight out
"Do you know a bird lives in here?"

And she said "yes" and smiled,
one or more birds do live in the store—
impossible to catch but sometimes
fed by the stockboys. I was so glad
she did not deny a bird
lives in my grocery. Such an omen!
So favorable! And she softened too
as she talked, so that the spectators—mostly
avocados, a few prunes,
relaxed their rigid lines and even the lady
arguing bottle returns was wont to smile.

And so I shopped. Up and down,
up and down the aisles with my head tilted back
to catch a sight of my own food bird.
And to hell with public health!
So a few droppings may land in the turnips—
they'll probably improve them.

I was afraid my looking up
would fool the public,
make them all look up
for Air Force One or the Goodyear Blimp,
or a sky message done by a romantic pilot,
and they'd get mad I'd gotten them to look
when, being in the supermarket, clearly
there could be no sky events above us
and they'd accuse me,
as if I am Chicken Little,
as if I am a false prophet.

# Signals for Prayer

Pock-marked snow in one lazy heap of shade,
haphazard dregs of winter and wasted
locked-in days are going in the lovely gutters.

I like dirty bits of paper,
muddied, ragged-paint porch steps,
the general ease of litter left,

the rag-tag yards and slovenly stoops
just plain in the sun.

And the legs released from winter. Lord,
let's us kick back and look the men over.

# Men

How I still do love them,
men who can't hold
eggs and weave
ropes with their fine silky hair
and hang themselves.
Men whose tongues lack talent
for the truculent luscious gums,
the hard individual teeth.
Men whose bodies
lumber up the hillsides
of women's bodies,
setting fire to shacks
where seedlings are started in the winter.
Can they help it
if thrust and parry
are all they know?
After the long slide of years
they will sit on park benches
and read the news,
which will seem important to them.

It's God's fault about men,
He gave them the long tool,
the fragile sac,
and placed them at their fronts
where they must be always
shielding from the blows.
And the wide shoulders
and hard diamonds of torsos,
the fabulous abundant hair
and the beards announcing
the regions below.
The poor sweet men are announcements

walking for God,
and their little buttocks,
the buttocks of babies,
and their big dumb feet.
And their eyes which try to hide
and cannot hide
God love em, so that the women
don't know whether to kill the men
or plant them,
carve them on crosses
or suckle them, the little fragrant goats.

# Making a Christ of the Average Jesus

Mary said to Jesus, Please, stay just one more day.
I'll serve stuffed grape leaves, finely-twisted challah
and those wonderful bitter olives you so love.
Jesus shut the door. He walked down the slender roadway,
really an alley, his nostrils chafing with smell
of the vendors' spices and their donkeys' dung.
He made his way to the lip of the Jezreel Valley.
Down the slanting mount he walked through the cedars
leaning north toward Nazareth, whence he had come.
The land was bristly and common, common scrub at its base.
Stone chains round the hillsides marked some paltry plots
along the road to Jaffa. Jesus' sandals stirred up dust
and it came to him—walking on water—as if above
the very element sorely missing in this land—
would be a telling coup. Figure the inland sea tides,
time of year, the angle of light toward dawn or dusk.
He knew it could be done. The fishermen would love it.
Gentiles would go for it too. In bright imaginings
Jesus walked for hours. Jaffa he was in before he knew it.
A driver stopped: did he want a lift to the beach? No,
he said, and drifted in the crowded stony city
piled on minor cliffs. Blisters formed on his heels.
His nose got sunburned and tender. The carcasses of lambs
hanging in the market were colorful all right
but God the flies! In a small smoky cafe, ceiling draped
in black homespun embroidered red and gold, Jesus
sat with a pastry. Honey dribbled onto his beard.
His demitasse of coffee was muddy as hell. Magdalene
said to meet her half past noon. She came in a black
caftan, heavy-breasted, hemline sagging badly.
Her face was lined and ashen. She had a hood engagingly
shadowing her face, making it all the more virginal,
all the more deathly. He told her his thoughts

on the coming campaign. She nodded, took notes,
she added insight there and here. His eyes got luminous
and lovey but Magdalene stayed on topic. Lights
were coming on by the time they finished their agenda—
the necessary betrayals, the ascension. The cock crowing
three times was a good final touch he thought.
Jesus was seeing his way clearer to how the stunted,
strict and galling could be told all milk and honey
when Magdalene asked, Have you spoken with your mother?
She and I have been talking. We say the schedule
of engagements should be intense—purposeful,
and meaningful, and go beyond the surface
straight to people's hearts. Therefore, she said, to a Jesus
nervous now in the corner—and soon to be taken aback—
therefore, Magdalene said, the nail holes will be real.

IV

# Multiple Sclerosis, the 13th Year of It

I put her on my back, carry her to the garden.
At the foot of a slope of pachysandra
spiked with lily of the valley, rose begonia,

I put the trowel in her hand, say Help me dig.
She digs a while and stops she is so tired.
She looks across the fence to the vacant lot.

She gets wall-eyed. Too cold there by the garden wall.
I carry her to the sun. I dig alone then,
transplants of ajuga purple-spotted as her feet.

I say Oh look at the sweet william.
She says only vaguely Yes. She doesn't care
for names or sun or shade. I lay my tools aside.

I put her on my back again. We move,
we come to a desert     I feel miles of hot sand
scorch my tongue and feet     she loves it, we're moving,
we move on through the desert for days,
for years     we come to rain forest: hot there too—steam
rises off the forest floor     she loves it there
we're moving     we come to a ravine     she thrills at the sight
of the long fall     I help her over the cliff     she's
moving on her own now     a pixie-haired woman: small,

blood-darkened feet. We're out for a motorized walk.
One foot falls heavily off and drags. She stops,
she lifts it back onto the wheelchair. It falls,

it falls again. Finally she says Oh let it be.
She tells me some cars try to kill her
when she crosses at the curb cuts

she's memorized in her part of the city. We buzz slowly
down the sidewalk, choose a movie by its wide doors,
a restaurant by its entryway that slopes.

# The Difference Between Me and Bill

Before he became a part of what is meant by
going belly-up,
back when he still wore suits and sold
business forms all over Hillsborough
County (Hell, all over
*Florida*, he'd say then),
he'd often grab a bite to eat
at a small luncheonette on Tampa Street,
sit near the plate glass window
and watch the demolition going on.
One day, the crane drops a girder and it neat
slices off the back of a man's head,
just like salami he tells me, and he's the first
and only one to see it happen. He feels it
isn't exactly fair for him to have to see it,
and it's only the beginning
of a long line of things he'll have to witness
though he doesn't leave the County,
and though his friends go on
to become magistrates, politicos,
simple kinds of moochers, while he goes
belly-up and watches his family fall away,
and I come to feel it isn't fair either,
it's not like my demolition.

In my demolition there's a house behind me
just filled with a trashy crowd.
Then the women and the children leave
and only a drunk guy and his buddies are left.
The heat and lights have long since been killed
so they tear off the mantel and the inner stairs
and burn them. They bring dogs to the house.
The dogs get mange, and the guy and his buddies

start to puke in broad daylight. Then the house
is condemned, the drunks are forced to move
and the city hires a crew to wreck the place.
It is a loud, graceful demolition
but somehow over quick,
the walls of the three stories
collapse against themselves
while sights as embarrassing as bathtubs,
as intimate as kitchen curtains,
come into everyone's view.
The last push before the final fall
produces, high above the heap
of what will soon be rubble,
an entirely alive, very fat raccoon
sitting on the back of a scarlet wing chair.
And it is surprised, and annoyed,
but not afraid. The raccoon escapes in time
and clearly she is a mamma raccoon, and that night
there is a moon over what is now a field.

# Last Fire: Letter to the Children Gone Away

Tonight I ready the house for the last
stacking logs, last fire.
I don't make a good fire by myself—
it burns too quickly,
or not at all, or scatters,
like us who lived here.

I will the fire to burn
evenly, without rancor,
without making fear of fire
out of bounds of hearth,
but the fire has a will of its own.

It was your father taught you
how to make a fire,
to lay the kindling twigs,
the quarter logs,
the big, slow-burning ones:
breathing on the whole
to make it start, watching for sparks
beyond the hearth, the safety of all of us.

And how to scatter the embers at bedtime,
close the iron screen,
and walk away.
By the time you left you could
each make several kinds of fire,
and name them too.

I still don't know the names of fires
your father taught you.
I was busy with cider,
hot chocolate and wine
and my own thoughts,
the safety of all of us.

I hope you remember too
I taught you some ways—
ways to lie before a fire with music
in the dark, listening to storms
and stories, how to tell them.

# Heard When His Daughter Told the Story

Across the Sound, in tandem with a Piper,
toward home from Mystic he was flying
his first solo, and at night, in snow.

I don't think he did that fall they do
in movies, when from a handsome formation
one plane banks off to the left, then another,

another—though he was capable of it—
he could fly. If he followed his left wing,
it was not from loving the flashiness

and flair of the act and the moment
wasn't revelatory, full of anything
so nameful as angels, or as dread. He wasn't

escaping, or making a point of failing.
He didn't mean to die without an ending—
no May Day, never a word.

If he banked on his nether side,
toward his diminutive, ice-covered wing,
it was because, alone in a small plane

in a snowstorm over the Atlantic,
he was trying to find his way.

# Questioning the Remains

The Gabriels left a white iron
bootscrape in the shape of a stalking cat
near the front porch steps, left a drying rack
for herbs or draping wicks of candles.

Out back's a lean-to where, the neighbors say,
Mr. Gabriel raised capons: cockerels
that grow fat and never mate or crow.
They say this was a cottage for Ruth Gabriel,

his bride. Did she pick the white glass chandelier,
shaped liked a nipple and grey-veined? Was the curved-
bottom porch swing here? Were the arm-thick white-washed
stones that hold the house taken from the ground around here?

What heavy thing made the floor in the east
by northeast bedroom slant so wildly west?

# Stepmother

Never has my boychild let me be
the sun. Never let me be the earth.
I'm the millstone for his childhood's century.
He runs through the carnival, leaving me
a shill for a family show
he didn't buy a ticket to.

Nights our old dog falls, though, and we must
help him, me and my half-grown son,
sometimes my boychild lets me be the moon,
lets his face collapse in the moonlight.

# My America That Divides

I once had campfires with my friend now gone
to Colorado: small campfires, small mountains
here in the East were all we had to offer.
She left for wilder parts.

Claudia can see Pike's Peak from her window
and it's true: not a half mile from her house,
some shaggy hills still shelter the coyote.
It's almost wild there.

Here, some yellow leaves lie pressing the old grass.
Mostly, leaves don't fall in Colorado.
Claudia looks through ponderosa pine in hip-deep snow
all winter, starting early, staying late.

I don't know what calls her there,
or whether she can remember that train sound
coming out of the black rock face in West Virginia:
Harper's Ferry. We camped there with our men and kids.

I love that place where the Potomac, that fast hard river,
and the muddy wide slow Shenandoah join.
In wildness, it's the best we have to offer.
Now some years have gone and on

her part of the continent, experts plot a hunt
so bison will not stray to the stranger richer grasses
out of range where they're allowed. On my part,
rain her land could use comes lightly down.

# The Darning Egg

How hard it was
to admit the matter
from the petri dish,
and have it then take root.

For hours she crouched on all fours,
then gently walked through the early days—
how not to jostle, or tire,
how to cradle a possible baby.

But in time, the miracle took. It made
three babies in her belly
and the doctor said: you have choices.
We can maybe

take one fetus, save
the others, make it
easier—possible—
for you to bear.

*Draw out from the womb*
*not "child" in the doctor's language*
*but "fetus," as in science,*
*a scientific thing,*
*a thing? Maybe hospitals*
*flush them, the gone ones?*
*They go down the buildings' gullets*
*to the sewers of the city*
*with the millions' other leavings*
*to be carried and carried*
*to the ocean: holy,*
*or not, but gone? Out there,*
*mainly, were there women*
*saying neither yes nor no,*
*but letting what would come, come?*

Her thoughts fly out and fly back.
Yet seeing two fledglings in a nest
she can't help being enthralled—
a joy is in it and she knows it, knows it

hard sometimes. By her window, the woman sits late.
With her right hand, she mends and makes new.
Wood in her other hand takes the needle,
and she draws up the thread, and she binds.

# All That Was Tendered

Joe and his roofers a long hot week
worked through the layers of shingle:
asbestos and boards and rusty nails,
the years' detritus came crashing.

Joe'd lovingly sheathed the laurel
—not a single branch was broken.
The white viburnum remained unscathed
and each night, with care, Joe shielded
the bare head of the house.

In the narrow stone throat of the driveway,
Joe backed in a large truck slowly.
The men hauled for several days.
Then over new pine planking,
in gently overlapping strokes,
Joe built a new red roof.

       *      *      *

The last day of the weeks of work
a man swung into her drive.
As he and Joe drank beer in the yard
she came to meet the stranger.

She talked with him a while,
then brought him *Carrying the Darkness:*
*The Poetry of the Vietnam War.*
She said "Take all the time you want.
Just bring it back here someday."

With nothing more to be said or done
she wrote Joe a check for the work.

       *      *      *

While at dusk she walked in the garden alone
Joe sat in his truck on the street.
He'd drink or talk to a passing buddy
and sometimes glance to her house,

to the fan-lit windows of her porch,
her chandelier's visible
opal globes. And he called
when the dark was near-complete,

"I did the job the best I could.
You didn't even know I was *there*."

# Lisa, with teacher

Lisa said, "They were flower children—hippies,
people from the sixties." Cocking her head
for some answer, and casting her eyes beyond me,
she said it as if, sharing her parents' generation,
I could explain her father murdering her mother,
that woman on her knees whose crown he shot away,
whose ear he tore off with his teeth. Explain
why he was freed on self-defense and Lisa's witness
made no difference, why it didn't count that she had seen
the ear on the floor, and the head's pulp spewing.
And why it didn't seem to matter that she'd cradled
the ruined crown all the way to the hospital,
and remembered her mother once saying
this is the most important part to shelter
when creatures are young. Lisa touched the auburn
profusion of her own crown as she brought me this,
and more, to answer, as if I could explain
how anything ever hardens, how anything ever heals.

# The Women Who Give Up Their Babies

Lonely to figure out and foist
their eager early wants on the world
they are barefoot to a bus and northsome gone.

In cities and towns and little crossroads
out in the country, anywheres not known
back home, they put their hands to work,

or drift, or go at things with a will.
They are just like everybody else:
clutter and empty pockets.

Years and miles from the child,
they hanker for risen rain
gone over the moon

south to downcounty.
A dry and damaged dark comes on.

V

# Sire

I rode with the cowboy
one night in a truck was all.
The actor I had in a cold house in the country
and the philosopher-king of the bar
got round me saying I was pretty,
serving me beer. He took me to deadend roads,
and cemeteries. We counted
whatever was above us—it was a galaxy
of near-truth, hair, nights
in that late November the stars were starving,
I was alone, I was a grey-eyed girl.

The actor has a ledge of brow, a furred gold
chest. The cowboy will be deeply tanned by now.
You'll know him by his bright saltwater eyes,
and if you have this
same gulf in your eyes, know you're his.
But if you're dark and tall,
if you like to ride wild
wherever a cycle may take you,
you'll be the barman's daughter.

# Gardening Where the Land Remembers War

My yard is just a small stockade
but I've planted my garden
heavily. A trumpet vine
falls on the northside fence
where barbed pyracantha climbs.
In the midst of snakeroot and hosta,
bugle, loosestrife, bleeding heart,
the stonecrop grows by bounds.

In the garden's bosom, the pivot,
stands one small dark red plum.

In a climate hard to survive
its red ups the ante in heat.
I didn't plant or intend it:
it preceded me in time.
To make my miniature plot of ground
appear a whole, made thing,
there's nothing to be done but with
red-tipped leaves—nandina, photinia,

the oakleaf hydrangea—echo
the red of the plum, recall it.

# The Cranesbill Sighted Everywhere

When fall comes to the garden,
the familiar cranesbill, its gaudy gore,

is the flower lasts longest of all:
yes *geranium*, upright or trailing—

anyone can own it.
In ordinary dirt of ground or pot

it thrives on the common touch,
and garners love by loving neglect.

To cultivate it is to just let be.
It makes no pretense to glory,

only by persistence in living makes glory.
And it's red: cranesbill can beckon you home.

# Old Southern Recipe

My mamma has a wide bosom,
her calf muscles tighten
like in a younger woman
dancer. She has fine plucked brows,
eyes blue in every light. Tough,
she never cries. She's the one
got me ready for this life
like you would a chicken
for the roaster: wring the neck,
remove the head,
let it run a while
then pluck it. The quills of some
tailfeathers will stay
embedded in the bumpy flesh.
Pluck it best you can
and cut out the giblets.
It's getting more fit to eat
now rub it with butter,
roast it slow. Boil the giblets
down for gravy. Sunday dinner,
sop it up. Go to the porch,
take up a picture of Jesus
mounted on a tongue depressor.
Fan a while. Mamma will cross her legs,
settle into what a drinker Daddy was,
or what a bitch Aunt Blanche has been
or how Lester caught three bullets
just when he was trying to straighten up
and do right TOO BAD.
She'll arch her foot to make a point.
Your starched white cotton blouse
will start to stick to the small of your back.
Mamma loves to preen her feet

while she settles into her subjects.
She'll arch her foot again, hold it,
you'll want to cry Aw let it go
but from the belly
of this three day visit
you read on the back of the fan *Behold,*
*everyone that useth proverbs*
*shall use this proverb against thee,*
*saying, As is the mother,*
*so is her daughter.*

# Country Song: White Chenille

Thing about her was the quick way
she turned her head,
deep-bosomed banty
Billy walked to with his eyes,
didn't even ask her to dance,
just looked at her all over.
Outside with hardly a word or time
he put blunt-fingered hands
on her breasts. Well Maggie was taken
with him. Cotton tufts were soft
that summer near Savannah, in 1929,
when Billy first lay Maggie down.

        *     *     *

When she brought him in the coffin
there were forty dark red roses in the woods
outside Macon, Georgia, April rain
and she was young in her
shantung dress, her bolero jacket.
The thicket of tall people standing round
said Billy's woman should look at her man.
Lifted up, she saw his fingers
grained with years of grease,
scarred with car parts falling,
saw him smoothed and powdered, man of hers
lay holding forty dark red roses.

        *     *     *

Now the bedspread's nubs are flattened
and sparse, Maggie hauls wash down
using it as tote.
Soon a pillowcase will do
for her few things.
And when she goes home to Georgia
in a box, funeral train
slow into her county,
I'll find that spread
and smooth it out and look:
the watery stains that show and prove
despite all bleach and care,
how many times, how many places
my daddy lay my mamma down.

# Polly Wadleigh Hay Smith Calling

Polly "lived in style"—
summer in La Jolla, winter in Hawaii,
long ways from Macon, Georgia, where she said
the heat got to her. Catfish Smith

the legendary football coach
jilted Polly in youth, then married her
in middle age. He might have been
a bottom feeder, or King of the Ocmulgee

(muddy water runs through Macon) or something
in-between: I just don't know. Don't know a thing
about The Hays of The Hay Mansion either.
These matters are distant and dim,

and Polly died last year. A few days before
she wrote me a letter, mostly about love
and pride. She said my daddy had been
handsome and fine and that she was

proud of us, and wished she could be with us all
some day, who like her came out of the deep
red clay along the Ocmulgee, and grew tough-
bottomed feet going barefoot most of the year.

(We had a phone wall unlikely to be painted
this lifetime, so the question came,
why not write on it?)
I can hear Polly answer *Wadleigh*,

the a that sounds like "ah,"
and the ending the "lay" in love
or down to sleep, with the ease
of respect and the history

we bear behind us, I can hear her calling
what spreads out over all of us—rich
or poor, famous or not, traveled
or stay-at-home—the family name.

# My People

My people came up out of the flat pine woods
and red clay gullies of Georgia. My people
had a way of centering themselves
in their hips, so that the men
would slightly bend their knees
and shift their legs a lot,
conscious of their sexes in their trousers,
those gabardine and khaki pants—workpants,
and the women would sway,
the women's moving started in their hips
and all their lives my people moved this way.

My people cooked—the spreads were huge—
ham and roast both on Sundays, biscuits,
green tomato pickle. Though they were
narrow-nostriled and fine-boned—
high foreheads, long fine necks—
like thoroughbreds, and they liked to think they
were thoroughbreds, but they weren't.
My people were as large as the world
in the work they did, and as small.
Like Uncle Sonny, he sold cars.
He had the bluest cracker eyes, big florid face,
and married to a piddling woman,
but he could tell a story.
He'd start by hiking up his pants,
and cracking first the knuckles on one hand,
and then the other. That's the extent of myth
in my people. They didn't do much bad or good.

There was one wild one—ran off to Atlanta,
studied dramatic acting and took off on a tour,
by train, traveled all the way to Iowa.

She got called back for a funeral,
had to come back to the woods
that all look alike,
and the talk so drawn-out
you could play a checker game
between Uncle Ashley's "Well" and his "I guess so."
For a while she ran with the crowds to tobacco balls,
had a bunch of beaus but then
quick and unexpected she married,
and kids came—more of my people,
and me. I envy mountains and the ethnics
and the Jews, and the black people of my country.
What my people are about
is nothing so wide or so deep.
My people just came up out of the flat pine woods,
and red clay gullies, of Georgia.

# The Big Bouquet of Talk

*to the talkers:*
*you know who you are*

One lady author says Mississippi people
repeat things: say the same thing twice.
Take a thing and say it one way, turn it
upside, shorten, lengthen, or gussy it up.
Why in the world she says this I don't know.
Don't have a clue why in hell but she does.
It's a bafflement, a paradox, and a puzzle.

Now you take Georgia. Person there might say
"You goin' to the post office? You goin' to town?"
—That's the same thing twice. Even up in New Jersey,
person crude in the way of talk might say
"Is the Pope Catholic? Does a bear shit in the woods?"
See what I mean? A person adding a flourish
or three—ruffle on the armchair of speech,

so to speak, fringe or satin tassel,
is not evidence of the same thing twice
entirely, or Mississippi marker. Besides,
with grace-note, more is more. It's how
relation is found or formed or what it is.
Take Georgia: whole state's related. Mamma'll be
on a train, and right away start talking.

Lady from Philadelphia turns out:
Georgia, born and raised. Talk to where a person
is from, even done drawn-out, clears
lighter, smaller stuff away, such as
"You got kids?" Or that modern version,
"What do you do?"—Silly question and not much
asked before the present now—people moving

all the time, so they've got to hang their hat
somewhere, and resort to the hook of *do*,
like this could describe or define them.
But Mamma, she goes for the jugular
central "Where you from?" And if it turns out
Georgia, she'll cut through cousins twice removed,
Aunt Lavinias and that Woodruff boy

she knew in '29 and pretty soon
the Philadelphia lady's related
some way, somehow. Always. Never seen it to fail.
Not blood relation every time, though Mamma
looks for that. I mean if we've both been
in Moultrie, or shared a friend in Waycross
or hell, milked a Wisconsin cow,

we've been down the same road and we know it.
Might wind around a lot: blind alleys,
offshoots, expansive, what have you. But
in that double handful, relation will be
got to: hard to grasp but true, believe me,
overblown, overgrown, trumped up or wild,
we're all live and needy and bound to die.

# ACKNOWLEDGMENTS

The author gratefully acknowledges the editors of the following publications, anthologies, and chapbooks in which some of these poems previously appeared: *Boulevard; Calliope; Chester H. Jones Foundation National Poetry Competition Winners 1989; Cimarron Review; Cincinnati Poetry Review; Contemporary New England Poetry: A Sampler, Vol. II* (Texas Review Press); *The Contemporary Review; Crossroads; Embers; Great River Review; Green Mountains Review; Heatherstone Poets & New Voices: Anniversary Edition* (Heatherstone Press); *The Hudson Review; The Iowa Source; The Journal; Karamu; The Laurel Review; Men & Women: Together & Alone* (The Spirit That Moves Us Press); *Negative Capability; New England Review & Bread Loaf Quarterly; The Onset Review; The Pennsylvania Review;* and *South Dakota Review.* Heatherstone Press in 1990 published the chapbook *A Gold Rain at Lonelyfarm,* which included seven of the poems in this collection; *The Painted Bride Quarterly* Chapbook Series in 1998 published *The Shine on Loss,* a chapbook which included six of the poems in this collection; Pudding House Publications in 2000 published *Greatest Hits,* which included twelve of the poems in this collection; Two Herons Press in 1992 published *Gardening Where the Land Remembers War,* a chapbook which included seven of the poems in this collection.

# ABOUT THE AUTHOR

Suzanne Rhodenbaugh was born in Florida to a Georgia family. After graduating from University of South Florida, she worked out of Atlanta and Washington, D.C., as an administrator for the early War on Poverty and related programs, and did farmwork on an Israeli kibbutz. She received an MPH in medical care administration from University of Michigan, and worked in western Pennsylvania for the United Mine Workers' health program, then did community organizing, health care consulting, and freelance writing and editing the years she was home with young children. She earned an MFA in writing from Vermont College and has taught writing for several Connecticut colleges, the Johns Hopkins Expository Writing Tutorial, and a Virginia school system. Her poems, essays, articles, and reviews have appeared in *The American Scholar, Cimarron Review, The Hudson Review, Michigan Quarterly Review, NER & BLQ, Salmagundi, St. Louis Post-Dispatch, The Washington Post, Utne Reader*, and other journals; in several anthologies; and in four chapbooks. She and her husband Tom live in St. Louis.

# RECENT BOOKS BY HELICON NINE EDITIONS

FICTION

*Jobs & Other Preoccupations*, a first collection of stories by Daniel Coshnear.
2000 Willa Cather Fiction Prizewinner. Introduction by Rosellen Brown.

*Toy Guns*, a first collection of short stories by Lisa Norris.
1999 Willa Cather Fiction Prizewinner. Selected by Al Young.

*One Girl*, a novel in stories by Sheila Kohler.
1998 Willa Cather Fiction Prizewinner. Selected by William Gass.

*Climbing the God Tree*, a novel in stories by Jaimee Wriston Colbert.
1997 Willa Cather Fiction Prizewinner. Selected by Dawn Raffel.

*Eternal City*, a first collection of stories by Molly Shapiro.
1996 Willa Cather Fiction Prizewinner. Selected by Hilary Masters.

*Knucklebones*, a first collection of short stories by Annabel Thomas.
1994 Willa Cather Fiction Prizewinner. Selected by Daniel Stern.

*Galaxy Girls:Wonder Women*, a first collection of stories by Anne Whitney Pierce.
1993 Willa Cather Fiction Prizewinner. Selected by Carolyn Doty. Second printing.

*Return to Sender*, a first novel by Ann Slegman, is both tender and hilarious.

*Italian Smoking Piece with Simultaneous Translation*, by Christy Sheffield-Sanford.
A multi-dimensional tour de force.

POETRY

*The Air Lost in Breathing*, a first book of poems by Simone Muench.
1999 Marianne Moore Poetry Prizewinner. Selected by Charlie Smith.

*Flesh*, a first book of poems by Susan Gubernat.
1998 Marianne Moore Poetry Prizewinner. Selected by Robert Phillips.

*Diasporadic*, a first book of poems by Patty Seyburn. Second printing.
1997 Marianne Moore Poetry Prizewinner. Selected by Molly Peacock.
2000 Notable Book Award winner for poetry (American Library Association).

*On Days Like This*, poems about baseball and life by the late Dan Quisenberry,
one of America's favorite pitchers.

*Prayers to the Other Life*, a first book of poems by Christopher Seid.
1996 Marianne Moore Poetry Prizewinner. Selected by David Ray.

*A Strange Heart*, a second book of poems by Jane O. Wayne. Second printing.
1995 Marianne Moore Poetry Prizewinner. Selected by James Tate. Received the
1996 Society of Midland Authors Poetry Competition Award.

*Without Warning*, a second book of poems by Elizabeth Goldring.
Co-published with BkMk Press, University of Missouri-Kansas City.

*Night Drawings*, a first book of poems by Marjorie Stelmach.
1994 Marianne Moore Poetry Prizewinner. Introduction by David Ignatow, judge.

*Wool Highways*, poems of New Zealand by David Ray. Received the
1993 William Carlos Williams Poetry Award (Poetry Society of America).

ANTHOLOGIES

*Spud Songs: An Anthology of Potato Poems*, edited by Gloria Vando & Robert Stewart.
Proceeds to benefit Hunger Relief.

*The Helicon Nine Reader: A Celebration of Women in the Arts*,
edited by Gloria Vando Hickok. The best of ten years of *Helicon Nine*.